PupStyle

TRICK OR TREAT

By Dara Foster

SCHOLASTIC INC.

New York   Toronto   London   Auckland
Sydney   Mexico City   New Delhi   Hong Kong

This book is dedicated to my loving daughters, Parker and Ripley

A special thank you to Melissa Gampel at DoggieCoutureShop.com
for her endless support and supply of costumes
and dog fashion accessories

Dog fashion styling, dog model casting,
photo shoot production and art direction by Dara Foster
Photography by Jonathan P. L. Spooner.

Credits:
Cover: Dogula costume by Puppy Love, dog model Delilah, dog groomer Jorge Bendersky; p. 3: bumblebee costume by Doggie Design, flower costume by Carlene Mahanna, dog models Emmet, Mei Mei, and Kiki Lu; pp. 5, 7: dog model Cooper; p. 7: raptor costume by Animal Planet; pp. 9, 11: dog model Lola; p. 11: costume by Deni Alexander Designs Inc.; pp. 13, 15: dog model Spanky, collar by Fetchers & Fighters Collars; p. 15: Harry Pawter costume by Dogo; pp. 17, 19: dog model Benjamin; p. 19: Sherlock Hound costume by Puppy Love; pp. 21, 23: dog model Tucker; p. 23: devil bat costume by Anit Accessories; pp. 25, 27: dog models Zara and Princess Giana; p. 27: spider dresses by Classy Doggie Designs by Linda Higgins; pp. 29, 31: dog model Mimi; p. 31: wig by Diva Pet, skeleton costume by Puppy Love, skull neck tie collar by Poochie Outfitters; pp. 33, 35: dog model Kanji; p. 35: rock star costume by Deni Alexander Designs Inc.; pp. 37, 39: dog model Mei Mei; p. 39: witch costume by Anit Accessories; pp. 41, 43: dog model Gia; p. 43: princess costume by Toni Mari, collar by Susan Lanci, tiara by Aria; pp. 45, 47: dog model Delilah, dog groomer Jorge Bendersky; p. 47: Dogula costume by Puppy Love; pp. 49, 51: dog model Gingi, dog groomer Jorge Bendersky; pp. 51: matador costume by Anit Accessories; p. 53, 55: dog model Louis; p. 55: Cutipillar costume by Zack & Zoey; pp. 57, 59: dog model Paddington; p. 59: mermaid costume by Casual Canine, wig by Wigglesdogwigs.com; pp. 61, 63: dog model Flo; p. 63: taco costume by Casual Canine, sombrero by Barking Baby; p. 64: ladybug tutu costume by KO Couture, necklace by PupStyle by Dara Foster, dog model Bizzie.

Backgrounds: p. 3: ISTOCKPHOTO; p. 7: ISTOCKPHOTO; p. 11: ISTOCKPHOTO; p. 15: SHIPOV PLEG/ SHUTTERSTOCK; p.19: IAKOV FILLMONOV/SHUTTERSTOCK; p. 23: SERGEY MIRONOV/SHUTTERSTOCK; p. 27: JENIFOTO/ SHUTTERSTOCK; p. 31: SANDRA CUNNINGHAM/SHUTTERSTOCK; p. 35: SHUTTERSTOCK; p. 39: ISTOCKPHOTO; p. 43: ISTOCKPHOTO; p. 47: WINSTON LINK/ SHUTTERSTOCK; p. 51: (street) ISTOCKPHOTO, (maracas) BLUEHAND/SHUTTERSTOCK; p. 55: JAG_CZ/SHUTTERSTOCK; p. 57: ISTOCKPHOTO; p. 63: SOFIAWORLD/ SHUTTERSTOCK.

ISBN 978-0-545-43676-2

12 11 10 9 8 7 6 5 4 3 2 1   12 13 14 15 16/0

Printed in Malaysia 106
First printing, September 2012

It's time for Halloween! Whether they're dressed as vampires or princesses, these doggies are looking for some treats!

There are approximately 150 types of dogs, called breeds. There are even more kinds of dogs that are mixed breeds, like this Schweenie, who is part schnauzer and part dachshund.

SCHWEENIE

Dinosaurs may no longer exist, but this puppy's outfit will never go out of style. Dogs have been man's best friend for over one thousand years. That's old but it's nothing compared to dinos, who lived 230 million years ago.

SCHWEENIE

Dogs are pack animals. This means they like to be in groups. Some packs can be made up of as few as two dogs. When you bring your dog home, you become a member of the pack too!

BULLDOG

Dogs called alpha dogs are leaders of their packs. This alpha bulldog queen is ready to rule with style.

BULLDOG

A veterinarian is a doctor for animals. They make sure dogs are healthy. It is important that dogs visit the veterinarian at least once a year.

BULL TERRIER

This wizard will cast a spell on you—
a cuteness spell! Just make sure he gives
you his pooch potion. It can turn you
from bow to wow!

BULL TERRIER

Some dogs have extra-good noses.
These dogs are used to track scents.
All dogs have a sense of smell that is
at least one thousand times stronger
than a human's.

BASSET HOUND

This basset hound detective is on the hunt for some canine clues. Some dogs have such a powerful tracking ability that they've discovered trails that are over a week old!

BASSET HOUND

Dogs can be a little naughty sometimes. They chew up couches, laundry, and shoes. But it's hard to stay mad for too long – they're too cute!

BOSTON TERRIER

This devilishly cute doggy's temp runs hotter than a human's. A dog's normal body temperature range is 100.5 to 102.5 degrees Fahrenheit. A human's is only around 98.6 degrees Fahrenheit.

BOSTON TERRIER

These Cavalier King Charles spaniels are worthy of royalty. In fact, they are named after a king named Charles!

CAVALIER KING
CHARLES SPANIEL

Many types of dogs were owned by rulers from all around the world. These pretty pooches are fit for a queen!

CAVALIER KING
CHARLES SPANIEL

It's no secret that dogs love bones. They love chewing on them, burying them, and digging them up again! But real bones can break apart and hurt a dog's mouth and belly. That's why it's important to give our pets dog treats instead of the real thing.

LONG-HAIRED CHIHUAHUA

Even though dogs can range in size from only a few inches tall to several feet, every dog has about 300 bones in his body. (A human has approximately 200.) This scary skeleton will have you shaking to the bone.

LONG-HAIRED
CHIHUAHUA

ost dogs can move their ears up, down, and side to side. That's because they have more than twice the amount of muscles in their ears than people.

CHINESE CRESTED

Some dogs have ears that stick up and some have ears that droop down. If a dog hears something, he will move his ears toward the sound to hear it better. It's no wonder this pup is a rock star – he can really hear the music.

CHINESE CRESTED

Witches aren't the only ones with spots! A dog's skin can be a range of colors, like brown, black, and pink. If a dog has spots on her skin, it does not always mean she has spots on her fur.

LONG-HAIRED CHIHUAHUA

This Chihuahua may not be able to see her future in this crystal ball, but it can be predicted that she'll be cute forever!

LONG-HAIRED CHIHUAHUA

Just like human fingerprints, no two
dogs have the same paw print.
But dogs even have another way to
identify themselves – their nose prints!
That's right: The pattern on a dog's nose
is different for every single dog.

PEEKAPOO

This cutie is a Peekapoo, which is a mix between a Pekingese and a poodle. Look out, paw-parazzi! This Peekapoo princess is ready for her close-up.

PEEKAPOO

A dog's bark can mean many things. They make noise when they're hungry, scared, excited, and sometimes to communicate with other dogs. Not every dog barks, though. In fact, some cannot bark at all!

POMERANIAN

Don't be afraid – Count Dog-ula
doesn't want to suck your blood, he just
wants all of your treats! What is
a vampire's favorite dog?
The bloodhound!

POMERANIAN

Dogs can be trained to do all sorts of tricks. If they're really good, owners can have them compete in contests. Competitions can be for speed, jumping, breed shows, and more.

MINIATURE
POODLE

Dogs get prizes for being the best in their category. This poodle is sure to be a cha-cha-champion.

MINIATURE POODLE

There are over 400 million dogs in the world. Dogs can be found on every continent.

LONG-HAIRED CHIHUAHUA

The country with the most dogs is the United States. One in every three homes has a canine companion. Who wouldn't want this snugglebug under their roof?

LONG-HAIRED
CHIHUAHUA

Not all pups can doggy paddle. Some are great swimmers, but others like to stay on dry land.

MORKIE

This Morkie mermaid is ready to explore the ocean. Hopefully she won't run into any *cat*fish!

MORKIE

Dogs that have parents both from the same breed are purebred. The Jack Russell terrier is an example of a purebred dog.

JACK RUSSELL TERRIER

No matter what the breed, all dogs are totally adorable, especially when they're in costumes! How do dogs feel on Halloween? Terrier-fied!

JACK RUSSELL TERRIER

HAPPY
HOWL-OWEEN!